SOUL STILL CALLING

Soul Sill Calling

by

Remin Devasia Josi

First Edition	: March 2025
Prepress Work	: Book Nest Publishing
Cover Design	: Sujith R.S.
Published by	: Book Nest Publishing
Press Work	: Repro India Ltd
Distribution Partner	: Repro India Ltd
Phone	: +91 94966 49547 | +91 96561 61635
Email	: booknestpub@gmail.com
ISBN	: 978-93-49488-33-5

This book is a work of fiction. Names, characters, places, and incidents are either products of the author's imagination or used fictitiously. Any resemblance to actual persons, living or dead, events, or locales is purely coincidental.

For permissions and inquiries, contact:
Book Nest Publishing
Phone : +91 97785 80700
Email : booknestpub@gmail.com

ISBN 9789349488335

9 789349 488335

Price : ₹ 200.00

SOUL STILL CALLING

Remin Devasia Josi

BOOK NEST PUBLISHING
THIRUVANANTHAPURAM

Remin Devasia Josi

Remin Devasia Josi is an aspiring Researcher, Data Enthusiast, and first-time Author whose writing is deeply shaped by personal experience and emotional honesty. He holds a Master's degree in Business Intelligence and Analytics from the University of Westminster, London, and a Bachelor's degree in Statistics from Government College Kariavattom, Kerala.

Born into a middle-class family in Kerala India, with a teacher for a mother, a Central Government employee for a father, and a sister settled in Abu Dhabi, Remin's life journey has been grounded in resilience, family values, and the pursuit of meaning beyond success.

Soul Still Calling—his debut memoir—is a heartfelt reflection on migration, loneliness, friendship, and finding home between two worlds. Through it, he writes not just to tell a story, but to leave behind a voice that many may recognize as their own.

Publisher's Note

Soul Still Calling is a heartfelt memoir that tells the story of a young man chasing his dreams abroad, facing unexpected challenges, and finding the strength to return home. Through honest words and emotional moments, Remin Devasia Josi shares an experience that many young people can relate to — the struggle between staying strong and feeling lost.

At Book Nest Publishing, we are proud to bring you this powerful and touching story. We hope it speaks to your heart and reminds you that every journey, even the painful ones, has meaning.

Warm regards,

Book Nest Publishing

Foreword

Some journeys don't end when the ticket is booked, the luggage is packed, or the flight lands. Some journeys live on — in memory, in dreams, and in the places where a piece of your heart quietly stayed behind.

This is not just the story of leaving home, chasing dreams, and returning with scars. It is the story of silence between goodbyes, the loneliness hidden behind smiling selfies, and the echo of a soul that still walks a rainy bridge in London. It's a story for every student who left with wide eyes and came back with heavy ones. For every friend who stayed when the world turned away. And for every person who asked, "Did I fail, or was this the only way forward?"

My work, Soul Still Calling not only broke me but healed me equally. I poured into these pages the truth I was too afraid to speak and the emotions that no caption could carry. This book is a tribute to the version of me that kept walking, even when it felt like everyone had stopped.

Most of all, this is for one person who stood beside me not just as a friend, but as a brother — the one who flew across countries, wiped away silent tears, and reminded me I wasn't alone even when the world tried to convince me otherwise.

If you have ever felt like your story was left unfinished, if your soul still calls to a place or a person long after you've left — then this book is for you.

May these words hold your hand, as they did mine.

— Remin Devasia Josi

If this book speaks to your heart, I'd love to see your moments with it.

Tag me and share your story using #SoulStillCalling on Instagram and let's carry each other's stories forward. (@_inventive_soul_)

Acknowledgments

This book would not exist without the strength, love, and light given to me by others.

To my family, thank you for loving me through every version of myself — especially the one that returned quieter, unsure, but grateful. Your unwavering support is the root of my resilience.

To my brother like friend— this story lives because you stood with me when everything else crumbled. From late-night talks to teary departures, from the Heathrow goodbye to the silent prayers afterward, you are the soul behind these chapters. Thank you for being my shield, my strength, and my reminder that all angels have no wings.

To my friends, both the ones who stayed and the ones who taught me by leaving — your presence, absence, and words shaped the emotions behind this book. Thank you for the lessons.

To the UK — your streets, your winters, your harsh realities and beautiful friendships — you changed me. You taught me how to walk through pain and still find moments of warmth. You gave me heartbreak, but also healing.

And to every reader, who turns these pages with empathy and an open heart — thank you. If you find even a sliver of your own journey within mine, then I have written something worthwhile.

This is not just my story. It is ours — for everyone who has left, returned, and still hears the soul calling.

Table of Contents

1. The Boy Who Dream London : 01

2. The Friend Who Came for Me : 07

3. From Monsoons to Misty Mornings : 12

4. A Room with Cold Walls : 17

5. Job Hunts, House Moves & Heartbeats : 22

6. Cracks Beneath the Surface : 27

7. The Loneliest Crowd : 33

8. Doors That Never Opened : 38

9. The Exit No One Saw Coming : 45

10. Home, But Not Whole : 52

11. Soul Still Calling : 59

Chapter 1

The Boy Who Dream London

Some kids in school dream cricket stadiums. Some wanted to be doctors, actors, or YouTubers with 1 million followers.

Me? I dreamed of London.

Not the touristy London with Big Ben or the one in Instagram reels with fancy filters. I dreamed of a quiet street, a chilly breeze, red double-decker buses passing slowly, and a boy — me — walking alone with a coat swinging on his shoulder like he belonged there. I didn't know much, but I could already feel that soft winter air brushing on my cheeks. I could almost smell the coffee from some small café in a corner of the city I'd never been to.

This wasn't a plan. It was a feeling. A deep one.

It all started in April 2018 — just after my 12th grade board exams. My classmates were planning trips to beaches, malls, or just watching movies to relax after all the tension. I was doing something very different that day.

There was a Study Abroad Fair happening at Taj Vivanta, Trivandrum. I didn't have a license to drive

TAJ VIVANTA
STUDY ABROAD FAIR

then, and my cycle wasn't an option unless I wanted to arrive there sweating like I ran a marathon. So, my father dropped me.

He was in a rush — already late for work. We didn't even have one of those deep father-son "good luck" talks. He just parked the scooter, handed me the file, adjusted his watch, and said, "Go inside, ask questions, don't just stand and smile at people. Call me if you finish early. I have meetings."

And off he went.

I walked into that hotel lobby like I was entering another planet. It smelled like expensive perfume and carpet shampoo. I was wearing a light blue shirt my mom ironed twice — one time before dinner the night before, and again at 6am because she said "the collar doesn't look sharp enough."

I felt nervous and a little out of place. Everyone around me looked so sure. Some students already had brochures. Some parents were taking notes. Me? I just stood near the UK stall because there was a poster of London Bridge — and something about it made me stop.

A woman from the booth smiled and said, "You could be studying here next year, you know."

I nodded. I wanted to say something smart back, but all that came out was, "Really?"

That moment stayed with me. Maybe it was her tone, maybe it was the photo, or maybe it was because for the first time, someone spoke about my dream like it could be real.

That one sentence made a home inside me. From that moment, my heart started quietly planning its own way to London.

But life had other plans too. My family wasn't against me studying abroad — they just thought it would be better if I did my bachelor's in Kerala first. And I agreed. I knew that rushing something so big wasn't the way. So, I joined BSc Statistics at Government College, Kariavattom.

The first year went smooth. I studied, made friends, had long bus rides, and life felt okay. But everything changed in my second year — when something none of us expected happened.

COVID-19.

One day we were in classrooms, and the next day, we were attending lectures from our beds, half-awake. Exams were postponed again and again. Plans were frozen. The whole world pressed pause. I was stuck.

The dream of London felt like it was slipping away. Slowly. Quietly. But I didn't give up.

I started visiting churches. Not just one. Many. I lit candles in different places, sat silently, and prayed for just one thing — "Let the door open. Let me go."

At home, I began looking up universities abroad. Late-night searches, endless tabs open, and a million thoughts in my head. I contacted study abroad agents — and faced everything from confusion to comedy. One agent said he would help with a UK course and then offered me something in Poland. Another told me Business Analytics was "like beauty therapy but with data."

I was half-laughing, half-panicking.

Then came the turning point.

I found Drisya from prestigious Study Abroad Company. She responded quickly. Calm, clear, and confident. "Hi Remin, I've checked your profile — yes, I can help."

Just those words gave me a sense of peace. She didn't promise shortcuts. She gave me a plan. Slowly, she helped me to shortlist universities. She explained everything properly and helped me to apply — even though my final-year exams hadn't been conducted yet.

Meanwhile, Kerala University was running its own show — with the timing of a 90s serial. They conducted Semester 4, 5, and 6 like back-to-back episodes, with no breaks. I still remember sitting in my room, writing one exam, taking a break, and then opening Netflix because I couldn't even process what subject was next.

It was exhausting. But in the middle of all that, I kept checking my emails — hoping for that one acceptance letter. I replied to everything on time, followed up, and sent documents even before I was asked. Every night, before sleeping, I imagined the streets of London again. That dream was my escape, my fuel.

Then came the big hit — the results were delayed. They were expected by May 2021 but got pushed to August. I missed the September intake.

That was a hard day. I didn't cry loudly. I didn't call anyone. I just lay down, stared at the ceiling, and let the silence speak.

But once again — Drisya didn't give up.

She said, "Let's defer to January. There's good news — the same course you wanted, MSc Business Intelligence and Analytics, is available at University of Westminster, London."

In that moment, it felt like the dream knocked on my door again. This time, more real than ever.

And just like that, after years of waiting, praying, exams, delays, agent dramas, and late-night dreaming... London was loading again.

Chapter 2

The Friend Who Came for Me

How he flew from the UK to Kerala — and how we began the journey together.

Let me introduce my brother like Friend. I call him "The Calm One." Not because he meditates or practices deep breathing (he doesn't), but because when I'm about to implode over minor stuff, like picking cereal, he's the guy who could watch the Titanic sink and say, "Don't worry, bro, we'll just build another ship."

We go way back — long before the UK chapter of my life. We bonded over late-night calls, food cravings that spanned continents, and dreams of escaping to something bigger. Something like... a university in London. When I finally told him about my visa submission in December 2021, I was on the verge of hyperventilating over the stack of documents that kept multiplying in front of me.

"Bro, I'm freaking out. My sister's wedding just ended, and now I've got this visa thing. I feel like I'm drowning in paperwork."

Without missing a beat, he replied, "Don't worry. I'll come. I'll fly to Kerala. We'll do this together."

Naturally, I thought he was joking. Why would he fly halfway across the world just to help me with a visa? But nope. He wasn't joking.

A few days later, he landed in Trivandrum like it was the most natural thing in the world. I was standing there, gaping, when I saw him walk out of the airport. "You just flew halfway across the world for me?" I asked, dumbfounded.

He smiled, shrugged, and said, "Why not? It's not about money, man. It's about moments. Besides, I kinda missed amma's Food."

At that point, I figured the universe had sent me a sign. I had someone by my side who wasn't just a friend, but a brother. Someone who would go to ridiculous lengths for me. Even if that meant flying halfway around the world for a visa submission.

We set off for Kochi for the VFS appointment — and, of course, I was a nervous wreck. I was checking my folder of documents every few minutes like I was about to lose my life's work. My friend, on the other hand, was sitting back like we were on a joyride to a beach, casually munching on snacks. No exaggeration, I'm pretty sure he had the entire train compartment's snack supply in his bag.

I asked, "Bro, what if they reject me? What if something goes wrong?"

He just looked at me, his eyes twinkling. "If they do, we'll start a shawarma shop next to Westminster. 'Remin's Wraps – Analytics Served Hot.'"

We both burst into laughter. And honestly, in that moment, the weight lifted off my shoulders. Sometimes, the best way to deal with something huge is to just laugh at it. And he knew that.

Fast forward to the next few days, and we were in full "Kerala prep mode." We hit every mall in Trivandrum. Lulu Mall? Check. Mall of Travancore? Check. We were ticking off every item on the "What you need in the UK" checklist — jackets, shoes, mugs, and a dozen other random things I probably didn't need, but someone thought I'd need.

Meanwhile, back home, amma was running her own operation — "Operation Pickle." She made three types of pickles, two kinds of masalas, and packed them all into tight jars like they were precious artifacts. You'd think she was preparing me for a nuclear apocalypse, not a long flight. And, of course, there was the homemade medicine in case I caught a cold in London. Because nothing says "home" like a jar of ginger-turmeric concoction.

Appa, in his usual way, took charge of the suitcase logistics — making sure the wheels were firmly attached, the locks worked, and that I wouldn't end up stranded in London because of a faulty bag. My sister's Husband give me a old British coin to keep it with me.

But none of this could distract me from the main thing hanging over my head — the visa.

It was December 19th when the call came in.

"Sir, parcel from VFS Global has arrived."

I could feel my heart in my throat. My friend was right there, as anxious as I was, but with a calmer exterior. We rushed to the courier hub in Trivandrum, my mind racing. As soon as the envelope was in my hands, I tore it open like it was the Holy Grail.

And there it was — my UK visa. Stamped. Approved. The dream was finally real. The weight of the past year — the uncertainty, the delays, the countless hours spent stressing over paperwork — suddenly vanished.

I looked at my friend. He was smiling, but his eyes told a different story. He knew what this meant. For both of us.

"We did it," I said, my voice barely above a whisper. "London, here we come."

And as we stood there in the middle of the bustling courier office, I realized something important. It wasn't just about the visa or the paperwork. It was about the people who show up when you need them the most. The ones who drop everything, fly across the world, and help you get one step closer to your dreams.

We walked out of that office, the world a little brighter, and our journey just beginning. I had my visa. And I had a friend who was with me every step of the way. A friend who would never let me forget that moments, not money, are what matter.

.*Chapter 3*

From Monsoons to Misty Mornings

***L**anding in the UK. The early days — excitement, confusion, and new air.r.*

December 25, 2021 — the night the dream finally took flight.

As the rest of the world celebrated Christmas with cake, carols, and cozy living rooms, I stood in the departure terminal of Trivandrum International Airport with a passport in one hand and silent prayers in the other. That night, while others celebrated the birth of Christ, I was stepping into a birth of my own — a new life, in a new country, with old fears hiding in my backpack.

It wasn't a coincidence that I chose to fly on Christmas Day. It was something I had imagined as a child — to take flight on this magical night. No reindeer, no sleigh. Just me, my passport, and a dream packed so tightly it almost hurt.

But I wasn't doing it alone.

Next to me stood my closest friend — not just a friend anymore, but a brother. He had flown all the way from London to Kerala just to be with me during my visa process. And now, he was flying back with me.

The same route, the same plane. But this time, I had him by my side.

My parents tried hard to hold it together. Amma gave me that smile — the one that tried to hide the tears already pooling in her eyes. Appa held my suitcase for just a few seconds longer than necessary.

As the plane took off, I looked through the window, eyes stinging slightly.

"Bro," my friend said, nudging me, "This is it. From monsoons to misty mornings."

And just like that, we left home.

The Emirates cabin felt like another world. Soft lighting, calm music, the occasional ding of seatbelt signs. I stared at everything — the screen, the tray table, even the remote — like it was part of a dream I didn't want to wake up from.

My friend looked at me and said, "Bro, don't press all the buttons. This is a flight, not NASA."

I smiled. That small joke kept me from overthinking.

During the Dubai layover, everything hit at once. The reality. The scale. The people. The sheer unfamiliarity. I clutched my documents tightly, scared I'd lose something important.

We sat near our gate, and suddenly, the tone of our conversation changed. He looked at me, not with his usual grin, but something deeper — something that felt like a father, a brother, and a best friend speaking all at once.

He said slowly, "From here on… anything happens, we'll be together. You hear me?"

"If you're scared, say it. If you don't understand, ask. Don't hold back."

"And if anything goes wrong, we face it. Together. We don't stay silent, bro. We speak. We fix. That's how we grow."

I didn't say anything at first. My throat was too full. I just nodded and held that sentence in my heart; like a shield.

In that moment, somewhere between two continents, I realized I didn't just have company on the journey — I had a brother for life.

When we landed at Heathrow, the first breath of UK air felt surreal. It wasn't warm. It wasn't even friendly. But it was new — and that was enough.

"Smells like possibilities and jet lag," my friend muttered, wrapping his jacket tighter.

The immigration line was long. My hands were sweating. I kept checking my folder — passport, CAS letter, TB certificate, bank statements — like they were a lifeline. When it was my turn, the officer glanced through my documents and asked, "Why are you here?"

I managed a small voice: "To study. University of Westminster."

He stamped the passport. "Welcome to the UK."

That sound — thump — meant everything.

I stepped out, my friend beside me, and said quietly, "So.. it's real?"

DEPARTURES

He replied, "It's as real as your mother's mango pickle. Let's go."

We were picked up by another friend, and together we headed to Littlestone, Kent — a quiet coastal town where we would spend five days in quarantine, as per the then-mandatory travel rules.

Kent wasn't London. It was sleepy, silent, and smelled of sea breeze and fog. But in that quietness, there was peace. A time to breathe. A pause between the life I'd left and the life I was walking into.

Those five days were filled with simple routines — cooking, unpacking, planning. At night, we'd sit by the window, sipping tea and talking about everything: the fear, the future, the family we missed.

And every now and then, that sentence would come back to me —

"From here on… anything happens, we'll be together."

In a world where everything was new — new air, new roads, new mornings — that sentence felt like home.

There was excitement — real, childlike excitement — of finally being here.

There was confusion — a constant whisper in my head asking, 'What now?'

And there was new air — cool, sharp, and full of untold stories.

The journey had just begun.

But I had a brother by my side.

And that made all the difference.

Chapter 4
A Room with Cold Walls

Settle Down. The emptiness behind the smiling selfies.

The quarantine in Littlestone ended quietly. Just two Indian boys, our bags slightly heavier with masalas and our minds still catching up to the fact that we were in a new country. For those five days, the air outside smelled different. The roads were too silent. Even the rain felt... foreign. But we had each other — two brothers trying to stay warm in the middle of a Kent winter.

Once quarantine was over, the real journey began.

We packed again — because apparently, life in the UK means always packing and unpacking. Our next destination: London. The city of my dreams, and also the city of "Sorry, the room is no longer available."

But before that, I had to collect my BRP (Biometric Residence Permit). An official card. A ticket to legally stay, work, and study. I remember walking into the post office with gloves on and nerves running wild. The lady at the counter looked like she'd handled a hundred BRPs that day, but when she handed mine over, it felt like a moment only I could feel.

"Welcome to the UK," she said.

I almost replied, "Thanks, I've waited four years for this."

Room hunting in London was like auditioning for a movie no one told you the plot of. Some rooms were too small, some landlords were too suspicious ("Do you plan to cook every day?" Yes, aunty, that's how survival works), and some rooms just smelled like heartbreak. After many failed attempts, we finally got a place in West Ham — barely a day before New Year's Eve.

We were exhausted, but hopeful.

"Bro," I told my friend, "We're going to start 2022 with a bang. Let's go to London Bridge. See the fireworks."

He smiled, "Let's make it unforgettable."

And oh — it was. Just not in the way we imagined.

Because 2022 started with a beautiful view of nothing.

The fireworks were cancelled. Some government decision. Crowd control. Safety measures. Call it what you want, but for me, it felt like life was playing a prank. I stood at London Bridge, wearing the coat I bought just for this night, watching the clock strike twelve... in silence. No lights. No boom. Just the cold, and a strange emptiness I hadn't expected.

The dream had arrived, yes. But it wasn't dressed the way I imagined.

We returned to the West Ham room, and at first, everything seemed fine. A decent housemate. Shared bills. But slowly, we realized one thing:

His friend was always around. And not in the "Hey, let's hang" way. More like "Who are these new brown guys in my kitchen?" way.

He wouldn't talk to us directly. But he'd stare. The passive kind. And being two brown boys just trying to warm our rice, we didn't feel safe.

One night, my friend whispered,

"Bro, this isn't it. We didn't fly across continents to feel like strangers in our own home."

I nodded. We knew it was time.

Luckily, my cousin stepped in like a guardian angel. She helped us find a new place in Croydon — a modest house, but with peace. And peace was gold.

That move felt like a second migration. New trains. New streets. New Google Maps confusions. But this time, we weren't scared. We were learning.

We began setting up our lives from scratch. Pots and pans. SIM cards. Amazon orders that took three days but felt like weeks. I still remember my first UK plug adapter. It felt like a medal.

We started exploring too. Hyde Park. Oxford Street. Shoreditch.

The smiles returned. And so did the selfies.

But here's the thing no one sees in those Instagram posts —

Behind every smile was a homesick boy pretending to be fine.

UNIVERSITY OF WESTMIINSTER

I finally went to my university — the University of Westminster. It was surreal. The glass doors. The ID card with my name printed perfectly. The campus didn't know the weight I carried. But as I walked through the halls, I told myself,

"You belong here. Don't let your smile lie to you."

My brother like friend still stood by me — cracking jokes, cooking late-night foods, saying things like:

"This is just the trailer, bro. The movie hasn't even started yet."

And I believed him. Because in that cold room, with its thin walls and creaky floorboards, something warm had begun —

A sense of becoming.

Chapter 5

Job Hunts, House Moves & Heartbeats

University life — from lecture halls to late-night breakdowns, from empty wallets to full hearts.

When I imagined university life in London, I saw libraries filled with smart-looking people, hot cups of coffee in cold hands, and a soft piano playing in the background — like a Netflix show.

Reality? Two days of online classes, one day of offline class, three days of stress, and seven days of "What am I even doing here?"

The first two weeks were rough. Not because of jet lag or cultural shock — but because the professors spoke faster than I could process. British speed + academic words = a deadly combo. I sat in class blinking like I was watching a cricket match in Japanese.

But slowly, things started making sense. I adapted. Listened more. Took notes like my life depended on it. And somehow… I understood.

At Westminster, I discovered that only four students (including me) were from India. Yes, just four of us — scattered in the crowd like coriander in a biriyani. But those three became my friends. We laughed, cried, submitted assignments together, and panicked over deadlines like in a war zone.

But not everything was rosy.

Some days I felt completely alone. I would return home after classes — to silence. No sound of Amma's kitchen, no smell of evening snacks, just walls. And sometimes, the walls echoed louder than voices. That's when I truly understood: this journey isn't just about degrees — it's about surviving your own mind.

The stress of assignments, group projects, and seminars piled up fast. The professors were lovely — supportive and engaging — but deadlines didn't care about feelings. I'd stay up past midnight with coffee that tasted like regret and curse every topic that began with "critically analyse."

And then came the biggest challenge of all: the hunt for a part-time job in London.

At first, it was fun — "Let's find a job and earn some pounds!"

But after 30 rejections and two interviews where I was ghosted harder than a bad Tinder date, the fun turned into frustration.

Croydon was far from central London, so one fine evening we shifted to Ilford, thanks to some sweet Senior Friends (Chettans – In Malayalam Language) we met at Stratford Mall — our unofficial job-hunting headquarters. These guys were friendly, funny, and practical. They had a double room vacant and welcomed us like family.

We cooked together, celebrated birthdays, and had our usual late-night therapy sessions:

"Bro, did you apply to Tesco?"

"Yeah. They said I need six years of experience in smiling."

"Try Pret. Maybe they just want five."

One memorable day, both of us cracked an interview at M&S in Stratford Mall. We celebrated early, thinking this was it — our breakthrough.

But two days later, the manager called:

"You both were great... but we hired someone else."

Someone else? We almost asked, "Who?

But no — just a random guy who apparently "fit the vibe better."

Still don't know what that means. Maybe we looked too desperate. Or too brown. We'll never know.

Finally, after months of struggle, I got temporary shifts — event jobs that meant 12 hours of running around stadiums and asking strangers if they wanted "crisps or water." Later, I worked as a kitchen assistant at The Grocer Pub. And yes — that meant washing plates while wondering what my MSc degree was doing.

I also became a Student Ambassador & Course Representative at Westminster — it was a proud moment. But the shifts were rare. And rent waits for no one. So, the financial pressure kept growing.

After four months of hustle and heartbreak, we made a big decision: let's move to Kent.

Why? Because a job as a Care Assistant opened up there. My university schedule was mostly flexible — just one offline class a week. So, it made sense.

We said goodbye to our Ilford Senior friends (Chettans – In Malayalam Language)— those warm, kind souls who fed us and kept us sane — and moved to Deal, Kent.

It was cold. Quiet. Different.

But it was also our new beginning.

The job in Kent was tough — but steady. And I was grateful. Finally, I felt the burden of joblessness lifting. Me and my brother like friend started exploring places again — Sandwich, Canterbury, Dover — and every place felt like a reward for surviving the storm.

Deadlines still existed. I still submitted one assignment literally 3 minutes before the portal closed.

But I was learning. Growing. Surviving.

At university, I made more friends. Some real, some just for group assignments. I smiled more. But behind the smiles… there were still quiet days. Mood crashes. Cravings for home.

Not all friendships were golden. Some people walked away; some showed their true colours when things got hard. That's when I learned:

You don't need many friends. Just one who stands with you — speaks when you stay silent, listens even when you pretend, you're fine.

And for me, that one… had flown all the way from the UK to Kerala, just to say:

"Anything happens from here on, we'll be together."

Still rings in my head. Still keeps me going.

Chapter 6

Cracks Beneath the Surface

The slow fade of friendships, the sting of silence, and the moments that quietly broke me.

Kent was supposed to be the restart we were hoping for. A quiet coastal town, new job, fresh faces. But even the quietest places can scream, and even the calmest air can carry a storm.

We'd been working as care assistants for about four months. The beginning felt hopeful—new uniforms, gentle smiles from elderly patients, the sense of purpose. But slowly, it began to rot beneath the surface. The pay came irregularly. One month, we got half. Next month, nothing. Two months went by—empty bank accounts, bills piling up, and not even an explanation.

Yet we stayed. We kept working. We kept hoping. We cooked noodles together and laughed in our small room, saying, "No more Sambhar, only British stew"

We thought maybe next week, next month, things would get better.

Then one day, it broke.

The care company owner, who once called me "like a son," turned his words into weapons. Out of nowhere, he accused me—said I had damaged the company car, said I had caused more loss than help, said I was a "troublemaker." But worse than the lies was the tone. Like I had always been a burden waiting to explode.

"You're the kind of guy who ruins everything," he said once.

I froze. I didn't know how to defend myself. I hadn't done anything. And still, people believed him—or stayed silent.

The final blow came when he filed a police case against me. Me—a boy who couldn't even raise his voice in an argument, now accused of damaging property and being morally corrupt.

He even twisted my friendships. He told others, "He only stays close to girls, just for attention."

As if kindness, support, or company needed to come with shame.

And suddenly, I wasn't just jobless. I was labelled.

The strangest thing about a false accusation is how quickly it wraps around your throat. Even those who know you, don't know what to say. They step back. They hesitate. They look at you differently, like wondering if the lie could be true.

That's when the real silence begins.

One day, I sat with my friend—the one who had flown from the UK to Kerala for my visa journey, the only one who still stood by me—and I asked, "Do you believe all this?"

He looked at me for a moment, leaned forward, and said with a voice that anchored me,

"I know your heart. That's enough for me. If the world turns its back, I won't."

That sentence stayed in my chest like a heartbeat.

But still, the damage was done. The town felt smaller, colder. We couldn't stay.

We decided to separate for a while. I moved to near Southampton, to live with some cousins. He moved near Bristol, to his family.

I thought a new place might heal things. I was wrong.

At first, my cousins welcomed me. Smiles, home-cooked meals, Malayalam conversations. But soon, behind closed doors, their words turned sharp. They told others I was a problem. That I had issues in Kent because of my behaviour. That my friend and I weren't really "good people."

They never said these things to my face. Only in whispers I could hear but never caught.

One night, I heard them say to someone on the phone, "I think He is not good"

I sat in the dark, phone in hand, heart collapsing in quiet thuds.

It wasn't just betrayal. It was betrayal by blood.

When I told my family everything, their words surprised me.

"Leave that place," my father said. "Go back to your friend. Some blood ties don't make family. Loyalty does."

I packed my bag the next day, walked out without looking back, and boarded a bus to Bournemouth as my brother like friend already shifted to Bourenmouth

When I arrived, my friend was waiting. No questions. Just a nod, a smile, and his hand grabbing my suitcase like old times.

Bournemouth was beautiful—seaside winds, chalk cliffs, and tourists laughing on the pier. It should have felt like peace.

But peace is not a place. It's a feeling.

We tried to rebuild. We met four other friends—Everyone was from Kerala—and took a flat together in Poole Hill. Six of us in total. Laughter returned in the form of jokes, late-night card games, cooking together.

But underneath it all, something had shifted.

No one ever said anything directly, but I could feel the judgement. The whispers from Kent had travelled. I was "that guy" now. The one with a past. A misunderstood image followed me like a shadow, one I couldn't scrub off.

Even in smiles, I sensed eyes checking me.

I once caught one of the guys staring at me and quickly looking away when I entered the room. The kitchen got quieter when I walked in. My presence didn't cause fear—but discomfort. And discomfort is its own kind of loneliness.

Still, I tried to stay strong.

We got another care job nearby. But after a while, they too said, "We need full-timers." I lost it again.

But finally, I landed a job at the Hilton Hotel in Bournemouth as a Food and Beverage Assistant. A job with dignity. With uniform. With appreciation.

I had survived another storm.

But little did I know — the biggest storm was coming from inside.

Chapter 7

The Loneliest Crowd

Living with people but feeling alone. When help vanished and words cut deep — I stopped pretending.

The flat in Poole Hill had six people, but it never felt more silent.

Every evening after my shift at the Hilton Hotel, I'd come home and hear voices—laughter, chatter, teasing. But the moment I stepped in, the air would tighten. Conversations would soften or change direction. I wasn't excluded. I just wasn't needed.

And there's something crueller about that than being rejected. It's the feeling that your absence or presence doesn't matter at all.

I wasn't the "funny one." I wasn't the "helpful one." I was the guy with a rumour attached to his name. The guy they'd heard about from someone who barely knew me. I wanted to shout, to explain, to cry even—but what would I say?

"Please believe I'm not who they say I am?"

"Please don't judge me for mistakes I never made?"

I couldn't say anything. So, I smiled. I cooked for everyone. I asked if anyone needed help. And then I sat quietly in my corner, pretending the cold wasn't crawling into my bones.

There's a difference between being alone and feeling alone. And here, I felt alone — constantly.

And then, one afternoon, I came home early from Hilton. I had walked all the way back, through the chilled wind near the sea, telling myself to stay strong. But when I reached the flat, it was empty. Everyone had gone to work.

I lay down to rest, eyes burning from exhaustion. Just a nap, I thought. But sleep took me too fast — and into a dream I can't forget.

It began in darkness. Not night — just a thick, heavy blackness. Then footsteps. Angry. Coming closer.

Suddenly, someone grabbed me. Pushed me. Beat me. I couldn't see their face — just a shadow, breathing heavily.

"You're the worst friend I've ever had,"

"You destroy everyone you meet."

"You'll die slowly — one piece at a time, just like you hurt others."

"You never belonged here. You are just an intruder."

His words pierced through skin and soul.

In the dream, I looked at my hand — it was bleeding. I begged, "Why are you doing this? What did I do?"

But there was no reply. Just more hitting. More words. More hatred.

It felt like the face belonged to someone I knew — but I couldn't see it. The shadow was familiar, but nameless. A ghost of my life.

Then suddenly I woke up, sweating. It was 8:14 p.m. The heater was off. The room was silent.

But my hands were still shaking.

I sat on the bed for what felt like hours. The nightmare had turned something inside me. And I couldn't shake the feeling — that the words might be true. That someone out there did think all this.

Worse — maybe everyone thought it, but didn't have the courage to say it to my face.

That night, I couldn't eat. I walked out to the corner shop, bought a Rubicon Jiuce, and stared at my reflection in the glass window.

"Am I really this hated?"

"Did I really come to the UK to end up like this?"

"Have I failed everyone? Am I even me anymore?"

I called my mother. I didn't say much, just asked how things were. But she could hear it.

"Son… are you okay?"

I paused. Then lied: "Yes. Just tired."

But something cracked in my voice. I could hear her swallow and her tears. She didn't ask more.

That night, I sat on my bed with my laptop open. My student visa was nearing its end. To apply for a stay-back visa, I needed at least £2000 in my account

— money I didn't have, and couldn't ask for. My job barely paid enough to cover rent. And savings? They had disappeared long ago into Oyster cards, groceries, and borrowed hope.

My dream of finding a job in Business Intelligence — it felt so far now. Companies weren't hiring international graduates like me. And even if they did, I had lost the energy to explain myself to one stranger, to hide one more pain behind a rehearsed smile.

So, I asked myself a question I'd never dared to before:

"Is it time to go back?"

The moment the thought came, my chest tightened.

Going back to India wasn't just a change of location. It was an admission. A stamp of failure.

People would ask, "Why are you back so soon?"

They'd assume I did something wrong. That I couldn't handle it.

They wouldn't know about the nights I went hungry.

The jobs I did. The betrayals. The fake friendships. The silent flatmates. The dream that bruised my soul.

I opened the browser. Logged in to the airline website. The date? Looking 1st week of May, 2023.

I clicked on a one-way ticket to Kerala.

And just before hitting "Confirm," I asked myself:

"Will anyone miss me?"

"Was this all for nothing?"

"Will the bridge in London remember my steps, even if no one else does?"

I didn't have the answers.

I still don't.

But I booked the ticket on May 7th 2023

And just like that, the journey that began with a dream was now headed back to the land I had once left behind — not because I wanted to, but because I had to.

Chapter 8

Doors That Never Opened

The search for a reason to stay. Emails unanswered, interviews that led nowhere — and the quiet ache of not being wanted where you once belonged.

It wasn't just the silence of friendships or the loneliness in rooms full of people or the dream which I saw that led me to that one-way ticket. There was something else too — something deeper, quieter, but just as painful. The truth that no one saw in my eyes: I couldn't find a way to stay. Not in the UK. Not in the way I had imagined.

I had come here with a goal — a dream — to build a career in data analytics. I had worked hard, studied harder. MSc in Business Intelligence and Analytics. A degree that sounded sharp, promising, global. I had seen myself in offices filled with screens and dashboards, making sense of numbers that moved markets and changed lives.

But the reality after graduation was far from the vision I had carried across oceans.

The UK job market didn't open its arms to me. I knocked on every door I could. Job portals became my daily ritual. LinkedIn felt like a second home — or maybe a battlefield. Every day, I tailored my CV, tweaked cover letters, and sent applications to roles that screamed "perfect match." Data analyst. Business intelligence developer. Junior analytics consultant.

And every day, rejection met me like a shadow.

Some replies were kind — "Thank you for applying, but…"

Most were silent — application seen, but never heard from again.

The clock was ticking. The post-study work visa wasn't forever. Two years, they had said. But those two years come with no guarantee — just a race against time. So I never look for Post study work visa rather I look for my field Job. I wasn't just looking for a job anymore. I was looking for sponsorship. A company that would not only hire me, but also say: "We believe in you enough to keep you."

But most companies in my field — tech, finance, analytics — either had no license to sponsor, or preferred candidates who were already eligible to stay long-term.

That's when the suggestion came in. "Why don't you try healthcare?"

"Care assistant jobs are in shortage list — they offer visas."

"You could work for 5 years, get your PR (permanent residency), and then switch to your field."

On paper, it sounded logical. A way to stay. A foot in the door.

But every time I imagined myself stepping into a care job — not because I wanted to, but because I had to — something inside me paused.

I spoke to professionals in the data field. A few kind mentors replied to my DMs.

One said, "Five years in a completely different industry? You may lose touch with your skills."

Another said, "It's hard to come back after that long, unless you keep actively working on your portfolio or projects."

And that's when the real question hit me:

"Will I still be me after five years?"

Would the boy who loved numbers and patterns and finding meaning in chaos still survive inside a uniform he never dreamed of wearing?

Would the version of me who fought so hard to get this degree… still be alive in five years if I gave up the very thing I came for?

Was survival worth it if it came at the cost of becoming someone I didn't recognise?

I remember one night — cold, late, and far too quiet — I sat with myself, no distractions, no screens. Just me, my heart, and this question that wouldn't leave:

"If I stay like this, will I still be proud of who I become?"

I knew many who had taken that path. Some stayed strong. Some made it work. But I also knew myself. And

I knew that pretending, just to survive, was already draining me in ways I couldn't explain.

Every job rejection felt like a personal blow.

Every "you're overqualified" from a retail store.

Every "we need someone who can commit long-term" from a tech company.

Every glance at my bank balance that didn't match my qualifications.

I had fought so hard — emotionally, academically, financially — to be here. And yet the door I came through now felt like a wall.

And in all of this, I wasn't alone. My friend — the one who had flown from the UK to India to help with my visa process — stayed beside me. He reminded me to breathe. Told me it would be okay. Pushed me to keep applying. When I broke down, he stood like a wall I could lean on.

But even he saw it — the tiredness behind my smile. The questions I couldn't answer anymore.

One evening, I looked at him and said, "I don't know who I'm becoming."

He didn't rush to answer. Just sat there, quiet, like he knew some questions don't need answers — just space.

We both knew I was slowly fading into someone I never planned to be.

I had one foot in the dream and one foot in despair.

And then came that breaking point.

The day I opened yet another rejection email, followed by a care home job post sent by someone trying to help.

I stared at both for a long time. One door closed. One I didn't want to walk through.

That night, I didn't sleep.

I thought of all the things that brought me here — the essays, the visa chaos, the flight on Christmas night, the photos, the rooms, the lectures, the interviews, the loneliness, the little wins, the breakdowns.

And somewhere in between, I quietly asked myself:

"Maybe leaving doesn't mean failing."

"Maybe going home is not giving up — maybe it's finding strength in not losing myself."

And that's how the decision began to form — not out of anger, not out of fear, but out of a deep, aching truth that whispered: "You tried."

I wanted to stay. I really did.

But not at the cost of my career, my identity, or my peace.

I couldn't keep waking up each day in a place that didn't see the value of what I brought to the table.

I couldn't keep explaining why I was good enough, begging for a chance to prove it.

And I couldn't keep lying to myself, saying "just five years" — when I knew those five years might take me farther away from who I was meant to be.

So I made the hardest decision I've ever made: I chose to go home.

Not because I was ready. But because staying meant slowly disappearing.

It was a decision built on months of confusion, hope, rejection, and questions no one could answer but me.

And as I looked at that booked ticket, I didn't cry out loud. But something inside me did break quietly.

It was the end of a chapter I never thought I'd write.

And yet... it was also the start of facing life on my own terms.

What I didn't know was how hard it would be to say goodbye.

Because while I was leaving the UK, a part of me — the dreamer, the believer — stayed behind on a rainy bridge in London, waiting.

Waiting for a day I might return.

Stronger.

Surer.

Ready not just to survive — but to thrive.

Chapter 9

The Exit No One Saw Coming

The ticket back to Kerala. The goodbye that felt unfinished. Standing in the rain on London Bridge, leaving more than just a city behind.

The decision wasn't made in a moment. It was built slowly, layer by painful layer, until the weight of it became unbearable. I didn't just wake up one day and decide to leave London. It was the silence, the injustice, the loneliness that settled like winter fog in my chest, the job issues. The dream that haunted me had been the final push, but the journey toward that decision had started much earlier.

This wasn't just a flight. It was a surrender. Or perhaps it was a rescue.

After everything that happened — the betrayal by the care company, the cruel false allegation, the way I was made to feel like a criminal instead of a student — I started seeing the city differently. Streets that once pulsed with promise now looked cold. Every job rejection, every unanswered email for visa sponsorships in my field, every ghosted opportunity in my own field felt like another quiet shove out the door.

I remember the night I booked the ticket. My hands were shaking. The flat was silent, except for the distant hum of traffic and the occasional creak from the old walls. I stared at my laptop screen like it was asking me to confess something.

"Are you sure you want to confirm your booking?"

No. I wasn't sure. How could I be? I had fought so hard to be here. I had waited years for this chance. But at some point, when everything around you break and no one notices — you start thinking maybe it's okay to stop fighting. Maybe it's okay to let go.

So, I clicked "Yes."

It was nearly 3 a.m. I didn't wake anyone. I just sat on my bed, staring at the confirmation email, my eyes burning with exhaustion. Outside my window, London blinked with indifferent lights. Life went on. It always does — with or without you.

The next morning, I told him. My brother. Not by blood, but by bond. The one who had flown back to India just to stand with me during my visa chaos. The one who told me on the flight to London, "Anything happens from here on, we'll be together."

When I said the words — "I booked my ticket back" — his reaction cracked something in me. He went quiet, his mouth slightly open, like he was waiting for a punch-line that never came. His face twisted with disbelief.

"You're going back? Just like that?" he asked, voice thick.

I nodded, unable to meet his eyes.

"Is this really how it ends?" he whispered.

Those words stayed with me.

We didn't speak for a long moment. Then he sat beside me, and we both broke down. Two men, two friends, trying to hold onto something while the world spun away beneath us. I told him everything — the dream, the fear, the sleepless nights, the visa struggles, the silent nights spent on bathroom floors crying because it was the only place no one could hear.

"I didn't come here to fail," I said, barely holding my voice steady. "But it's like the more I try, the more I lose. I've lost my peace, my sleep, my self-worth. And now, I feel like I'm losing myself."

He didn't try to stop me. Maybe because he understood. Maybe because he knew, deep down, that I had reached the edge of something no one else could see.

The next day, we went shopping. I had saved a bit of money from my last pay checks. Not much, but enough to buy something small for my family. I walked through the aisles of the store as if in a daze, selecting small gifts that felt like apologies. I had left with dreams. I was returning with stories I couldn't even explain. This wasn't how it was supposed to go.

He walked beside me the entire time — quiet, present. I could feel his heartbreak mirroring mine. He had been my anchor in this foreign land, and now, I was cutting the rope. But even then, he stood with me. Just like he always had.

At home, we packed my bags together. Every shirt, every paper, every tiny reminder of my time here went into those bags. But what couldn't fit was the heaviness inside my heart. The dreams I was leaving behind. The part of me that had started becoming London — slowly, painfully — now being torn away.

That night, before the flight, we barely slept. We talked, laughed quietly, and kept pausing in between sentences, like our voices knew this was the last time they'd echo in the same room. Every laugh ended in a silence that said, "I'll miss you."

Morning came too quickly. We made our way to the bus station. The ride to Heathrow was surreal. I stared out the window and saw the city blur past — West Ham, Stratford, Ilford, Croydon, even London Bridge where the New Year had disappointed me just a year before. Each place was a chapter. A heartbeat. A memory.

My heart whispered goodbye to every turn. Goodbye to cold winter nights and hopeful summer walks. Goodbye to job interviews that ended in silence. Goodbye to libraries that held my stress and cafés that knew my tears. Goodbye to the streets that had seen me at my worst, and occasionally, my best.

But the hardest goodbye? It was to him. The friend who stood by me when the world felt too heavy. Who reminded me that I was worth something even when everything around me screamed otherwise. Who, in this final act, refused to let me feel alone.

At Heathrow, we didn't say much. There were no dramatic hugs, no film-like breakdowns. Just silence. A sacred kind of silence that wrapped around both of us like a final promise.

As I stood at the check-in counter, I looked at my suitcase. It was lighter than when I had arrived. But it carried more than just clothes. It held every rejection, every hope, every bruise, every tear I had poured into this journey.

I didn't take a selfie. I didn't post a "farewell London" story. This wasn't for the world to see. It was too sacred, too raw. Some exits can't be filtered. Some heartbreaks deserve to be grieved in silence.

He looked at me one last time and said, "Call me when you land. No matter the time."

I nodded, trying not to let my face crumple.

"I'm proud of you," he added. "You fought longer than most would have."

I turned to go, but my steps felt heavy. I paused, looked back one last time, and tried to smile.

Then I whispered — mostly to myself — "You gave it everything. Even when it gave you nothing back."

As I walked into the terminal, a strange calm settled over me. Not peace, not yet — but a kind of acceptance. That sometimes, bravery isn't in staying. Sometimes, it's in knowing when to go.

And London?

London didn't flinch. It didn't pause. It didn't whisper goodbye.

But I did.

I whispered it to the city. To the life I built. To the broken pieces I couldn't carry. And to the boy who had arrived here with dreams, now walking away with lessons carved deep into his soul.

This wasn't the ending I had imagined.

But maybe — just maybe — it was the one I needed.

Chapter 10

Home, But Not Whole

Back in the land I left — but I wasn't the same. The silence around my story, the loss no one saw, and the soul still reaching across oceans.

The moment the plane touched down in Trivandrum, a lump settled in my throat.

I looked out the small oval window — the trees, the faded airport buildings, the familiar grey sky — everything I had once longed for when I was alone in my UK rooms. But now, seeing it again, I felt a hollowness I couldn't name.

I didn't smile.

I didn't cry.

I just sat there, frozen, as the seatbelt sign blinked off and passengers began rising around me.

I had come back.

But I didn't feel like I had arrived.

The flight from London had been a blur of unspoken goodbyes. I remembered standing at Heathrow, my brother like friend beside me, both of us too drained to speak. He had tried to hold it together, just like me. But I could feel it in the way his eyes welled up again, in the silence that followed every hug, in the way our handshake turned into one last embrace — as if both of us knew this wasn't just a farewell. It was the closing of a book neither of us wanted to finish reading.

As I walked into Trivandrum airport, there was no dramatic return. No music playing in my head, no cinematic reunion. Just the humid air wrapping around me like a heavy blanket, and a single word pulsing through my chest:

"Now what?"

My family was waiting outside, faces full of love, relief, and expectation. I hugged them tight. My mother's eyes glistened as she whispered, "My son is back." My father tried to hide his emotion, standing still, smiling through tired eyes.

To them, I had returned from the UK.

But they didn't know that parts of me were still scattered across London pavements.

Still sitting in that empty Stratford bus stop.

Still sleeping on a couch in Cousin's House.

Still crying silently into a pillow in Bournemouth, trying not to wake anyone.

The days that followed were filled with gentle chaos — relatives dropping by, neighbours waving, cousins asking questions that I had no strength to answer properly.

"How was London?"

"You'll go again, right?"

"Didn't you get a job there?"

"Must have been amazing! All that freedom, all that opportunity!"

I smiled. I nodded. I lied.

Because how do you explain that coming back doesn't always mean returning? That a piece of your spirit stayed back in a place that never really claimed you? That you feel like an intruder even in your own home because the version of you that left — hopeful, strong, innocent — didn't return?

No one asked why I looked different.

Why my laugh sounded thinner.

Why I paused before answering even the simplest questions.

Why I avoided looking at old photos.

Why sometimes I excused myself in the middle of conversations and just stood alone outside, watching the clouds and wondering what London looked like at that moment.

Home felt familiar — but not comforting.

It felt like life had carried on here in loops — unchanged, unmoved — while I had been twisted into a thousand shapes, broken, rearranged, and then dropped back into this old setting like a piece that no longer fit.

There were nights when I would lie in bed, staring at the ceiling fan, letting it whirl my thoughts round and round.

I would think about my friend — my brother — and our last conversation before I left.

The way he told me, "You don't have to prove anything anymore. You tried more than anyone ever could."

And I had cried again — not out of sadness, but because someone had finally said it.

Back in Kerala, no one said that.

Not because they didn't care, but because they didn't know how.

Was it worth leaving everything behind to chase a dream that never gave me a real chance to breathe?

Was it worth the tears, the rejections, the betrayals, the near arrests, the nights spent wondering if I'd ever feel normal again?

I had wanted to bring back a story of triumph — something my city, my friends, my parents could proudly share. But all I brought back were scars hidden beneath a polite smile.

I tried getting back to work. Helped around the house. Visited a few relatives. Went to a cousin's wedding. Listened to people complain about the price of petrol and the heat and the elections. And all the while, I smiled. I laughed when I was supposed to.

But inside, there was a quiet rage.

Not at them — but at life.

At how easily it all unravelled.

At how quickly the world moved on while I was still catching my breath from the fall.

I still kept my UK sim card active — as if some part of me hoped I'd get one call. From someone. Anyone. Telling me that maybe, just maybe, I could come back. That it wasn't really over.

But the phone stayed silent.

Some days, I revisited old photos. Not to relive them, but to remind myself that it did happen. That it wasn't just a long, vivid dream.

The selfie with my first Oyster card.

The blurry shot on Christmas night at London Bridge — where there were no fireworks, just cold wind and the sound of laughter from strangers.

The day I passed the M&S interview. The evening, I walked out of that jobless, knowing someone else got it instead.

The night I cooked rice with just Curd only because that's all I could afford.

The day I booked my return ticket, silently, without telling anyone — because that's how my story was ending: quietly, unceremoniously.

There were moments I almost forgot it all. When my mother made biryani. When the rain hit our rooftop in a familiar rhythm. When my old friend stopped to talk with me. For a second, I felt warmth.

But then night came.

And with it, silence.

And in that silence, I remembered everything again.

I would lie awake, sometimes clutching the hoodie I brought back — the one I used to wear on my way to lectures. It still smelled faintly of London's cold.

And I would close my eyes and whisper —

"Did I fail? Or did life just not give me a fair chance?"

I still don't know the answer.

But I do know this:

I didn't come back empty.

I came back with stories untold.

With grief carried like invisible luggage.

With a strength I never knew I had — because it takes strength to walk away when your heart wants to stay.

It takes strength to say goodbye to a version of you that fought so hard.

And so, even though I returned to Kerala, to my house, my people, my soil —

I returned different.

Quieter.

Tired.

But not broken.

Because somewhere in the stillness, I know — my story isn't over.

It just took a detour.

A pause.

A breath.

And even if the world never sees the weight of what I carried back, even if no one ever asks the full truth —

I know.

And maybe, someday, the version of me still standing on London Bridge in the rain will find peace too.

Chapter 11

Soul Still Calling

I'm here — but my soul still walks that rainy bridge in London, waiting.

Some stories don't end with a period.

They end with a pause — the kind that holds your breath hostage.

I came back to Kerala with the kind of silence that echoes louder than words.

People said, "You're home now. You should be happy."

But no one knew that every time I looked at the sky, I saw clouds shaped like old British buildings.

That every time I heard the rain, it sounded like London.

My body was here — back in the land that raised me.

But my soul?

My soul never boarded that flight.

It stayed behind — still standing on that rainy bridge, where the lights of London flickered like unspoken dreams,

Still waiting for something — maybe healing, maybe an answer, or maybe just... peace.

I tried to move on.

I got busy again.

Work, responsibilities, smiles for the people around me.

But deep down, I knew — this wasn't closure.

It was camouflage.

Some nights, I hear it — the call.

Not from a person. Not from a job. Not even from a city.

But from the version of me I left behind.

The boy who cried silently on the flight.

The one who bought gifts on his last day, trying to act normal while his heart was breaking.

The one who once stood on a street in Croydon with empty pockets and stubborn hope.

He still walks through my dreams — sometimes wearing a backpack, sometimes wearing pain like a second skin.

And every time I hear that call, I remember…

The smell of the air when it rained in London.

The cold that bit through my jacket and into my bones.

The voices of people I no longer speak to.

The kindness of strangers.

The betrayal of ones I trusted.

The weight of trying to survive when the world turned its back.

London didn't just give me memories.

It gave me scars with stories.

Stories I couldn't tell when I first came back.

Stories people still wouldn't understand if I tried.

Because how do you explain to someone that a city broke you… and still feels like home?

This book is my attempt to do that.

To put into words what my eyes couldn't show and my smile tried to hide.

To honour the part of me that fell apart, alone and unseen, in the middle of a crowd.

To finally give voice to the version of me who stopped pretending.

But the truth is — even now — I'm still not sure where my home truly is.

Kerala gave me roots.

London gave me wings.

And somewhere between those two, I lost the map.

There are days I walk along the beaches here and wonder if the waves ever carried my story back across the ocean.

If the wind that rushes past me remembers how I once stood on Westminster Bridge, praying not to disappear into silence.

If the soul I left behind still waits for me under a grey sky, holding the pieces I couldn't carry home.

People ask me, "Will you go back?"

And I always answer with a smile.

But inside, I whisper,

"I never truly left."

Because that soul —

That boy —

That dreamer —

Still walks that rainy bridge.

Still looking at the city lights.

Still hoping for a different ending.

Still calling out to me through time and memory, saying:

"Come finish what we started."

And maybe one day… I will.

Maybe one day, I'll board a flight not out of desperation, but out of peace.

Maybe I'll return not to chase dreams, but to reunite with the parts of me that never moved on.

Maybe I'll Walk those same streets again — not as a broken boy, but as a whole man.

But until then —

I live with the echo.

With the ache that never dulls.

With the images that flash behind closed eyes.

With the memory of December rain and borrowed jackets.

With the gratitude for those who stayed, and the grief for those who didn't.

I'm here — in the land that calls me by name.

But a part of me still answers to another rhythm.

A city that saw me at my worst, and in some strange way, gave me the strength to become my truest self.

This story doesn't have a happy ending.

It doesn't even have a neat one.

Because some stories don't end with closure.

They end with continuation.

With echoes.

With souls that still call.

And if you listen closely — if you've ever stood at the crossroads between where you came from and who you became —

You'll understand why, even now…

My soul is still calling.

BIN TRAVERLER FORM

#16

Cut By: Edymar Berris Qty 73 Date 09-18

Scanned By: ____________ Qty ______ Date ______

Scanned Batch ID's

____________ ____________ ____________

Notes / Exceptions

____